WILLIAM MILLER

Herald of the blessed hope

WILLIAM MILLER

Herald of the blessed hope

The story of William Miller and his followers is traced through the time of their great disappointment in 1844, their subsequent discovery of what really happened on that day, and their renewed hope as by faith they looked ahead to the ultimate victory of God's people at Christ's return.

Compiled From the Writings of Ellen G. White

REVIEW AND HERALD® PUBLISHING ASSOCIATION
HAGERSTOWN, MD 21740

This book was
Edited by Gerald Wheeler
Cover design by Warren Rood
Typeset: 11/13 Sabon

PRINTED IN U.S.A.

99 98 97 96 95 94   10 9 8 7 6 5 4 3 2 1

R&H Cataloging Service
White, Ellen Gould (Harmon), 1827-1915.
    William Miller: herald of the blessed hope.

    1. Miller, William, 1782-1849. 2. Millerite
movement. I. Title.

                    [B]
                [286.709]

ISBN 0-8280-0853-1

Contents

Prologue

"We need to experience just such a reformation as was experienced in the time of William Miller's preaching. Many, fearful that they would not get a seat, would come for miles, bringing their food with them, and would remain all day to the meetings. I want to see such days again" — (*General Conference Bulletin,* May 31, 1909).

William Miller 1782 - 1849

Historical Foreword

Ever since the first advent of Christ, from time to time religious revivalists have appeared with urgent appeals to prepare for His promised second coming. Some of these appeals have originated from wild speculation. By contrast, William Miller based his message on careful Bible study and interpretation. And though he missed an important element, which produced the Great Disappointment, his plea for people to be ready for Christ's coming is still timely and important.

In the spirit of the prophetic messengers of the Bible, Miller was humble but firm in his conviction that he had a message of great importance. While the religious world around him was largely complacent about the Second Advent, assigning it to the far-distant future, Miller confidently expected it to occur in the lifetime of his hearers.

Miller's proclamation produced a great spiritual revival. Perhaps as many as 100,000 people responded to it. His audiences heard at least two things from him: first, that Jesus is a personal Friend and Saviour who cares about every individual; second, that He is coming very soon, and we need to be ready. As Miller put it, we are to be "continually prepared" for the Advent. These same messages are relevant and needed today.

William Miller, the first of 16 children, was born to William and Paulina Miller on February 15, 1782, at Pittsfield, Massachusetts. Though he received only 18 months of formal schooling, his thirst for knowledge drove him to a level of self-education far beyond the average for his time. Turning from his vocations of farming and justice of the peace between 1831 and 1844, he preached throughout the northeastern United States. It was a turbulent period in American history that included conflict over slavery, a temperance reform movement, and rapid westward expansion of the country.

Miller died December 20, 1849, having done all he could to help prepare the world for Christ's soon return. He was buried in a small country cemetery in Low Hampton, New York. His grave may seem lonely and forgotten, but it is not. "Angels watch the precious dust of this servant of God, and he will come forth at the sound of the last trump" (*Early Writings*, p. 258).

In presenting this compilation from Ellen White's writings, the White Estate Trustees hope that you, the reader, will sense anew the urgency of preparing for Christ's return, as well as the excitement of being in heaven with Him.

CHAPTER ONE

Skeptic Turned Preacher

An upright, honest-hearted farmer, who had been led to doubt the divine authority of the Scriptures, yet who sincerely desired to know the truth, was the man chosen of God to proclaim the nearness of Christ's second coming. Like many other reformers, William Miller had in early life battled with poverty, and had thus learned the great lessons of energy and self-denial. [1]

The members of the family from which he sprang were characterized by an independent, liberty-loving spirit, by capability of endurance, and ardent patriotism—traits which were also prominent in his character. His father was a captain in the army of the Revolution, and to the sacrifices which he made in the struggles and sufferings of that stormy period may be traced the straitened circumstances of Miller's early life. He had a sound physical constitution, and even in childhood gave evidence of more than ordinary intellectual strength. [2]

His mind was active and well-developed, and he had a keen thirst for knowledge. Though he had not enjoyed the advantages of a collegiate education, his love of study and a habit of careful thought and close criticism rendered him a man of sound judgment and comprehensive views.

He possessed an irreproachable moral character and an enviable reputation, being generally esteemed for his integrity, thrift, and benevolence. [3]

By dint of energy and application he early acquired a competence, though his habits of study were still maintained. He filled various civil and military offices with credit, and the avenues to wealth and honor seemed wide open to him.

His mother was a woman of sterling piety, and in childhood he had been subject to religious impressions. In early childhood, however, he was thrown into the society of deists, whose influence was the stronger from the fact that they were mostly good citizens and men of humane and benevolent disposition. . . . By association with these men, Miller was led to adopt their sentiments. The current interpretations of Scripture presented difficulties which seemed to him insurmountable; yet his new belief, while setting aside the Bible, offered nothing better to take its place, and he remained far from satisfied. He continued to hold these views . . . for about twelve years. [4]

At the age of thirty-four, however, the Holy Spirit impressed his heart with a sense of his condition as a sinner. He found in his former belief no assurance of happiness beyond the grave. The future was dark and gloomy. Referring afterward to his feelings at this time, he said:

"Annihilation was a cold and chilling thought, and accountability was sure destruction to all. The heavens were as brass over my head, and the earth as iron under my feet. Eternity—what was it? And death—why was it? The more I reasoned, the further I was from demonstration. The more I thought, the more scattered were my conclusions. I tried to stop thinking; but my thoughts would not be controlled. I was truly wretched, but did not understand the cause. I murmured and complained, but knew not of whom. I knew that there was a wrong, but knew not where or how to find the right. I mourned, but without hope."

In this state he continued for some months. "Suddenly," he says, "the character of a Saviour was vividly impressed upon my mind. It seemed that there might be a being so good and compassionate as to himself atone for our transgressions, and thereby save us from suffering the penalty of sin. I immediately felt how lovely such a being must be, and imagined that I could cast myself into the arms of, and trust in the mercy of, such a One. But the question arose, How can it be proved that such a being does exist? Aside from the Bible, I found that I could get no evidence of the existence of such a Saviour, or even of a future state."

"I saw that the Bible did bring to view just such a Saviour as I needed; and I was perplexed to find how an uninspired book should develop principles so perfectly adapted to the wants of a fallen world. I was constrained to admit that the Scriptures must be a revelation from God. They became my delight; and in Jesus I found a friend. The Saviour became to me the chiefest among ten thousand; and the Scriptures, which before were dark and contradictory, now became a lamp to my feet and a light to my path. My mind became settled and satisfied. I found the Lord God to be a Rock in the midst of the ocean of life. The Bible now became my chief study, and I can truly say, I searched it with great delight. I found the half was never told me. I wondered why I had not seen its beauty and glory before, and marveled that I could ever have rejected it. I found everything revealed that my heart could desire, and a remedy for every disease of the soul. I lost all taste for other reading, and applied my heart to get wisdom from God."

He now publicly professed his faith in the religion which he had despised. But his infidel associates were not slow to bring forward all those arguments which he himself had often urged against the divine authority of the Scriptures. He was not then prepared to answer them; but he reasoned that if the Bible is a revelation from God, it must be consistent with itself; and that as it was given for man's instruction, it must be adapted to his understanding. He determined to study the Scriptures for himself, and ascertain if every apparent con-tradiction could not be harmonized.

Endeavoring to lay aside all preconceived opinions, and

dispensing with commentaries, he compared scripture with scripture by the aid of the marginal references and the concordance. He pursued his study in a regular and methodical manner; beginning with Genesis, and reading verse by verse, he proceeded no faster than the meaning of the several passages so unfolded as to leave him free from all embarrassment. When he found anything obscure, it was his custom to compare it with every other text which seemed to have any reference to the matter under consideration. Every word was permitted to have its proper bearing upon the subject of the text, and if his view of it harmonized with every collateral passage, it ceased to be a difficulty. Thus whenever he met with a passage hard to be understood, he found an explanation in some other portion of the Scriptures. As he studied with earnest prayer for divine enlightenment, that which had before appeared dark to his understanding was made clear. He experienced the truth of the psalmist's words, "The entrance of thy words giveth light; it giveth understanding unto the simple" (Ps. 119:130).

After two years of careful investigation, he was fully satisfied that the Bible is its own interpreter; that it is a system of revealed truths so clearly and simply given that the wayfaring man, though a fool, need not err therein; that "all scripture is given by inspiration of God, and is profitable for doctrine, for reproof, for correction, for instruction in righteousness" (2 Tim. 3:16); that "prophecy came not in old time by the will of man; but holy men of God spake as they were moved by the Holy Ghost" (2 Peter 1:21); that it was written "for our learning, that we through patience and comfort of the scriptures might have hope" (Rom 15:4).

With intense interest he studied the books of Daniel and the Revelation, employing the same principles of interpretation as in the other scriptures, and found, to his great joy, that the prophetic symbols could be understood. Angels of heaven were guiding his mind, and opening to his understanding prophecies which had ever been dark to God's people. Link after link of the chain of truth rewarded his efforts; step by step he traced down the great lines of prophecy, until he reached the solemn conclusion that in a few years the Son of God would come the second time, in power and glory, and that the events connected with that coming and the close of human probation would take place about the year 1843. [5]

With a new and deeper earnestness, Miller continued the examination of the prophecies, whole nights as well as days being devoted to the study of what now appeared of such stupendous importance and all-absorbing interest. [6]

Entering upon the study of the Scriptures as he had done, in order to prove that they were a revelation from God, Miller had not, at the outset, the slightest expectation of reaching the conclusion at which he had now arrived. He himself could hardly credit the results of his investigation. But the Scripture evidence was too clear and forcible to be set aside.

He had devoted two years to the study of the Bible, when, in 1818, he reached the solemn conviction that in about twenty-five years Christ would appear for the redemption of His people. "I need not speak," says Miller, "of the joy that filled my heart in view of the delightful prospect, nor of the ardent longings of my soul for a participation in the joys of the redeemed. The Bible was now to me a new book. It was indeed a feast of reason; all that was dark, mystical, or obscure to me in its teachings had been dissipated from my mind before the clear light that now dawned from its sacred pages; and, oh, how bright and glorious the truth appeared! All the contradictions and inconsistencies I had before found in the Word were gone; and although there were many portions of which I was not satisfied I had a full understanding, yet so much light had emanated from it to the illumination of my before darkened mind, that I felt a delight in studying the Scripture which I had not before supposed could be derived from its teachings." [7]

Deeply impressed by these momentous truths, he felt that it was his duty to give the warning to the world. He expected to encounter opposition from the ungodly, but was confident that all Christians would rejoice in the hope of meeting the Saviour whom they professed to love. His only fear was that in their great joy at the prospect of glorious deliverance, so soon to be consummated, many would receive the doctrine without sufficiently examining the Scriptures in demonstration of its truth. He therefore hesitated to present it, lest he should be in error, and be the means of misleading others. He was thus led to review the evidences in support of the conclusions at which he had arrived, and to consider carefully every difficulty which presented itself to his mind. He found that objections vanished before the light of God's Word, as mist before the rays of the sun. Five years spent thus left him fully convinced of the correctness of his position.

And now the duty of making known to others what he believed to be so clearly taught in the Scriptures urged itself with new force upon him. "When I was about my business," he said, "it was continually ringing in my ears, Go and tell the world of their danger. This text was constantly occurring to me: 'When I say unto the wicked, O wicked man, thou shalt surely die; if thou dost not speak to warn the wicked from his way, that wicked man shall die in his iniquity; but his blood will I require at thine hand. Nevertheless, if thou warn the wicked of his way to turn from it; if he do not turn from his way, he shall die in his iniquity; but thou hast delivered thy soul' (Eze. 33:8, 9). I felt that if the wicked could be effectually warned, multitudes of them would repent; and that if they were not warned, their blood might be required at my hand."

He began to present his views in private as he had opportunity, praying that some minister might feel their force and devote himself to their promulgation. But he could not banish the conviction that he had a personal duty to perform in giving the warning. The words were ever recurring to his mind, "Go and tell it to the world; their blood will I require at thy hand." For nine years he waited, the burden still pressing upon his soul, until in 1831 he for the first time publicly gave the reasons of his faith. [8]

---

[1] *The Spirit of Prophecy,* vol. 4, p. 202.
[2] *The Great Controversy,* p. 317.
[3] *The Great Controversy,* vol. 4, p. 202.
[4] *The Great Controversy,* pp. 317, 318.
[5] *The Spirit of Prophecy,* vol. 4, pp. 202-206.
[6] *The Great Controversy,* p. 325.
[7] *Ibid.,* p. 329.
[8] *The Spirit of Prophecy,* vol. 4, pp. 206, 207.

CHAPTER TWO

Beginning to Witness

As Elisha was called from following his oxen in the field, to receive the mantle of consecration to the prophetic office, so was William Miller called to leave his plow, and open to the people the mysteries of the kingdom of God. With trembling he entered upon his work, leading his hearers down, step by step, through the prophetic periods to the second appearing of Christ. With every effort he gained strength and courage as he saw the widespread interest excited by his words. [1]

It was only at the solicitation of his brethren, in whose words he heard the call of God, that Miller consented to present his views in public. He was now fifty years of age, unaccustomed to public speaking, and burdened with a sense of unfitness for the work before him. But from the first his labors were blessed in a remarkable manner to the salvation of souls. His first lecture was followed by a religious awakening in which thirteen entire families, with the exception of two persons, were converted. He was immediately urged to speak in other places, and in nearly every place his labor resulted in a revival of the work of God. Sinners were converted, Christians were roused to greater consecration, and deists and infidels were led to acknowledge the truth of the Bible and the Christian religion. . . . His preaching was calculated to arouse the public mind to the great things of religion and to check the growing worldliness and sensuality of the age.

In nearly every town there were scores, in some, hundreds, converted as a result of his preaching. In many places Protestant churches of nearly all denominations were thrown open to him, and the invitations to labor usually came from the ministers of the several congregations. It was his invariable rule not to labor in any place to which he had not been invited, yet he soon found himself unable to comply with half the requests that poured in upon him.

Many who did not accept his views as to the exact time of the Second Advent were convinced of the certainty and nearness of Christ's coming and their need of preparation. In some of the large cities his work produced a marked impression. Liquor dealers abandoned the traffic and turned their shops into meeting rooms; gambling dens were broken up; infidels, deists, Universalists, and even the most abandoned profligates were reformed, some of whom had not entered a house of worship for years. Prayer meetings were established by the various denominations, in different quarters, at almost every hour, businessmen assembling at midday for prayer and praise. There was no extravagant excitement, but an almost universal solemnity on the minds of the people. His work, like that of the early reformers, tended rather to convince the understanding and arouse the conscience than merely to excite the emotions.

In 1833 Miller received a license to preach from the Baptist Church, of which he was a member. A large number of the ministers of his denomination also approved his work, and it was with their formal sanction that he continued his labors. He traveled and preached unceasingly, though his personal labors were confined principally to the New England and Middle States. For several years his expenses were met wholly from his own private purse, and he never afterward received enough to meet the expense of travel to the places where he was invited. Thus his public labors, so far from being a pecuniary benefit, were a heavy tax upon his property, which gradually diminished during this period of his life. He was the father of a large family, but as they were all frugal and industrious, his farm sufficed for their maintenance as well as his own. [2]

Though he had little of the learning of the schools, he became wise because he connected himself with the Source of wisdom. He possessed strong mental powers, united with true kindness of heart, Christian humility, calmness, and self-control. He was a man of sterling worth, who could not but command respect and esteem wherever integrity of character and moral excellence were valued. He was attentive and affable to all, ready to listen to the opinions of others, and to weigh their arguments. Without passion or excitement he tested all theories and doctrines by the Word of God; and his sound reasoning, and intimate knowledge of the Scriptures, enabled him to refute error and expose falsehood. [3]

---

[1] *The Spirit of Prophecy,* vol. 4, pp. 207, 208.
[2] *The Great Controversy,* pp. 331, 332.
[3] *The Spirit of Prophecy,* vol. 4, p. 208.

MR. MILLER'S LATE RESIDENCE

CHAPTER THREE

The Work Grows

Those who believed that the Advent movement was of God went forth, as did Luther and his colaborers, with their Bibles in their hands, and with fearless firmness met the opposition of the world's great teachers. Many to whom the people had looked for instruction in divine things were proved to be ignorant both of the Scriptures and of the power of God. Yet their very ignorance rendered them more determined; they could not maintain their position by the Scriptures, and they were driven to resort to the sayings and doctrines of men, to the traditions of the Fathers.

But the Word of God was the only testimony accepted by the advocates of truth. "The Bible and the Bible only" was their watchword. The weakness of all arguments brought against them revealed to Adventists the strength of the foundation upon which they stood. At the same time it angered their opponents, who, for want of stronger weapons, resorted to personal abuse. Grave doctors of divinity sneered at William Miller as an unlearned and feeble adversary. Because he explained the visions of Daniel and John, he was denounced as a man of fanciful ideas, who made visions and dreams his hobby. The plainest statements of Bible facts, which could not be controverted, were met with the cry of heresy, ignorance, stupidity, insolence.

Many churches were thrown open to the enemies of the Advent faith, while they were closed against its friends. [1]

Again and again did William Miller urge that if his doctrine were false, he should be shown his error from the Scriptures. In an address to Christians of all denominations

PLATE I. THE IMAGE OF DANIEL II.

he wrote: "What have we believed that we have not been commanded to believe by the Word of God, which you yourselves allow is the rule and the only rule of our faith and practice? What have we done that should call down such virulent denunciations against us from pulpit and press, and give you just cause to exclude us (Adventists) from your churches and fellowship?" "If we are wrong, pray show us wherein consists our wrong. Show us from the Word of God that we are in error; we have had ridicule enough; that can never convince us that we are in the wrong; the Word of God alone can change our views. Our conclusions have been formed deliberately and prayerfully, as we have seen the evidence in the Scriptures."

At a later date he stated: "I have candidly weighed the objections advanced against these views; but I have seen no arguments that were sustained by the Scriptures that, in my opinion, invalidated my position. I cannot, therefore, conscientiously refrain from looking for my Lord, or from exhorting my fellowmen, as I have opportunity, to be in readiness for that event."

In a letter to a friend and fellow-laborer, he spoke thus: "I could not see that I should harm my fellowmen, even supposing the event should not take place at the time specified; for it is a command of our Saviour to look for it, watch, expect it, and be ready. Then, if I could by any means, in accordance with God's Word, persuade men to believe in a crucified, risen, and coming Saviour, I felt it would have a bearing on the everlasting welfare and happiness of such. I had not a distant thought of disturbing our churches, ministers, religious editors, or departing from the best biblical commentaries or rules which had been recommended for the study of the Scriptures. And even to this day, my opposers have not been able to show where I have departed from any rule laid down by our old standard writers of the Protestant faith. I have only interpreted Scripture in accordance with their rules." [2]

While drawing crowded houses of intelligent and attentive hearers, Miller's name was seldom mentioned by the religious press except by way of ridicule or denunciation. [3]

Instead of arguments from the Scriptures, the opponents of the Advent faith chose to employ ridicule and scoffing. . . . The gray-headed man who had left a comfortable home to travel at his own expense from city to city, from town to village, toiling unceasingly to bear to the world the solemn warning of the judgment near, was sneeringly denounced as a fanatic, a liar, a speculating knave.

Time, means, and talents were employed in misrepresenting and maligning Adventists, in exciting prejudice against them, and holding them up to public contempt. Ministers occupied themselves in gathering up damaging reports, absurd and malicious fabrications, and dealing them out from the pulpit. Earnest were the efforts put forth to draw away the minds of the people from the subject of the Second Advent. But in seeking to crush out Adventism, the popular ministry undermined faith in the Word of God. It was made to appear a sin, something of which men should be ashamed, to study the prophecies which relate to the coming of Christ and the end of the world. This teaching made men infidels, and many took license to walk after their own ungodly lusts. Then the authors of the evil charged it all upon Adventists. . . .

The great controversy between truth and error has been carried forward from century to century since the Fall of man. God and angels, and those united with them, have been inviting, urging men to repentance and holiness and Heaven; while Satan and his angels, and men inspired by them, have been opposing every effort to benefit and save the fallen race. William Miller was disturbing Satan's kingdom, and the arch-enemy sought not only to counteract the effect of the message, but to destroy the messenger himself. As Father Miller[4] made a practical application of Scripture truth to the hearts of his hearers, the rage of professed Christians was kindled against him, even as the anger of the Jews was excited against Christ and His apostles. Church members stirred up the baser classes, and upon several occasions enemies plotted to take his life as he should leave the place of meeting. But holy angels were in the throng, and one of these, in the form of a man, took the arm of this servant of the Lord, and led him in safety from the angry mob. His work was not yet done, and Satan and his emissaries were disappointed in their purpose.

Comparing his own expectations as to the effect of his preaching with the manner in which it had been received by the religious world, William Miller said: "It is true, but not wonderful, when we become acquainted with the state and corruption of the present age, . . . that I have met with great opposition from the pulpit and professed religious press; and I have been instrumental, through the preaching of the Advent doctrine, of making it quite manifest that not a few of our theological teachers are infidels in disguise. I cannot for a moment believe that denying the resurrection of the body, or the return of Christ to this earth, or a judgment day yet future, is any the less infidelity now than it was in the days of infidel France; and yet who does not know that these things are as common as pulpits and presses are? And which of these questions are not publicly denied in our pulpits, and by the writers and editors of the public papers?

"Surely, we have fallen on strange times. I expected, of course, the doctrine of Christ's speedy coming would be opposed by infidels, blasphemers, drunkards, gamblers, and the like; but I did not expect that ministers of the gospel and professors of religion would unite with characters of the above description, at stores and public places, in ridiculing the solemn doctrine of the second advent. Many who were not professors of religion have affirmed to me these facts, and say they have seen them and have felt their blood chilled at the sight.

"These are some of the effects which are produced by preaching this solemn and soul-stirring doctrine among our Pharisees of the present day. Is it possible that such ministers and members are obeying God, and watching and praying for His glorious appearing, while they join these scoffers in their unholy and ungodly remarks? If Christ does come, where must they appear? And what a dreadful account they will meet in that tremendous hour!"

It is the lot of God's servants to suffer opposition and reproach from their contemporaries. Now, as in the time of our Saviour, men build the sepulchers and sound the praises of the dead prophets, while they persecute the living messengers of the Most High. William Miller was despised and hated by the ungodly and unbelieving; but his influence and his labors were a blessing to the world. Under his preaching, thousands of sinners were converted, backsliders were reclaimed, and multitudes were led to study the Scriptures and to find in them a beauty and glory before unknown. [5]

---

[1] *The Spirit of Prophecy,* vol. 4, pp. 212, 213.
[2] *Ibid.,* pp. 217, 218.
[3] *The Great Controversy,* p. 336.
[4] "Father" is used here as a term of respect.
[5] *The Spirit of Prophecy,* vol. 4, pp. 218-221.

CHAPTER FOUR

Preaching the Judgment

The prophecy of the first angel's message, brought to view in Revelation 14, found its fulfillment in the Advent movement of 1840-1844. In both Europe and America, men of faith and prayer were deeply moved as their attention was called to the prophecies, and, tracing down the Inspired Record, they saw convincing evidence that the end of all things was at hand. The Spirit of God urged His servants to give the warning. Far and wide spread the message of the everlasting gospel, "Fear God, and give glory to him; for the hour of his judgment is come" (Rev. 14:7).

Wherever missionaries had penetrated, were sent the glad tidings of Christ's speedy return. In different lands were found isolated bodies of Christians, who, solely by the study of the Scriptures, had arrived at the belief that the Saviour's advent was near. In some portions of Europe, where the laws were so oppressive as to forbid the preaching of the Advent doctrine, little children were impelled to declare it, and many listened to the solemn warning.

To William Miller and his colaborers it was given to preach the message in America, and the light kindled by their labors shone out to distant lands. The testimony of the Scriptures pointing to the coming of Christ in 1843 awakened widespread interest. Many were convinced that the arguments from the prophetic periods were correct, and, sacrificing their pride of opinion, they joyfully received the truth. Some ministers laid aside their sectarian views and feelings, left their salaries and their churches, and united in proclaiming the coming of Jesus. There were but few ministers, however, who would accept this message; therefore it was largely committed to humble laymen. Farmers left their fields, mechanics their tools, traders their merchandise, professional men their positions; and yet the number of workers was small in comparison with the work to be accomplished. The condition of an ungodly church and a world lying in wickedness burdened the souls of the true watchmen, and they willingly endured toil, privation, and suffering that they might call men to repentance unto salvation. [1]

PORTRAIT OF WILLIAM MILLER

The people were moved everywhere the message reached them. Sinners repented, wept, and prayed for forgiveness, and those whose lives had been marked with dishonesty were anxious to make restitution.

Parents felt the deepest solicitude for their children. Those who received the message labored with their unconverted friends and relatives, and with their souls bowed with the weight of the solemn message, warned and entreated them to prepare for the coming of the Son of man. Those cases were the most hardened that would not yield to such a weight of evidence set home by heartfelt warnings. This soul-purifying work led the affections away from worldly things, to a consecration never before experienced. Thousands were led to embrace the truth preached by William Miller, and servants of God were raised up in the spirit and power of Elijah to proclaim the message. [2]

Though opposed by Satan, the work went steadily forward, and the Advent truth was accepted by many thousands.

Everywhere was heard the searching testimony warning sinners, both worldlings and church members, to flee from the wrath to come. Like John the Baptist, the forerunner of Christ, the preachers laid the ax at the root of the tree, and urged all to bring forth fruit meet for repentance. Their stirring appeals were in marked contrast to the assurances of peace and safety that were heard from popular pulpits; and wherever the message was given, it moved the people. The simple, direct testimony of the Scriptures, set home by the power of the Holy Spirit, brought a weight of conviction which few were able wholly to resist. Professors of religion were roused from their false security. They saw their backslidings, their worldliness and unbelief, their pride and selfishness. Many sought the Lord with repentance and humiliation. The affections that had so long clung to earthly things they now fixed upon heaven. The Spirit of God rested upon them, and with hearts softened and subdued they joined to sound the cry "Fear God, and give glory to him; for the hour of his judgment is come." [3]

[1] *The Spirit of Prophecy,* vol. 4, pp. 222, 223.
[2] *Spiritual Gifts,* vol. 1, pp. 133, 134.
[3] *The Spirit of Prophecy,* vol. 4, pp. 223, 224.

CHAPTER FIVE

Pleading With Sinners

In March 1840 William Miller visited Portland, Maine, and gave a course of lectures on the second coming of Christ. These lectures produced a great sensation, and the Christian church on Casco Street, where the discourses were given, was crowded day and night. No wild excitement attended the meetings, but a deep solemnity pervaded the minds of those who heard. Not only was a great interest manifested in the city, but the country people flocked in day after day, bringing their lunch baskets, and remaining from morning until the close of the evening meeting.

In company with my friends, I attended these meetings. Mr. Miller traced down the prophecies with an exactness that struck conviction to the hearts of his hearers. He dwelt upon the prophetic periods, and brought many proofs to strengthen his position. Then his solemn and powerful appeals and admonitions to those who were unprepared held the crowds as if spellbound. . . .

Special meetings were appointed where sinners might have an opportunity to seek their Saviour and prepare for the fearful events soon to take place. Terror and conviction spread through the entire city. Prayer meetings were established, and there was a general awakening among the various denominations; for they all felt more or less the influence that proceeded from the teaching of the near coming of Christ. [1]

In June 1842 Mr. Miller gave his second course of lectures at the Casco Street church in Portland. I felt it a great privilege to attend these lectures; for I had fallen under discouragements, and did not feel prepared to meet my Saviour. This second course created much more excitement in the city than the first. With few exceptions, the different denominations closed the doors of their churches against Mr. Miller. Many discourses from the various pulpits sought to expose the alleged fanatical errors of the lecturer; but crowds of anxious listeners attended his meetings, and many were unable to enter the house. The congregations were unusually quiet and attentive.

Mr. Miller's manner of preaching was not flowery or oratorical, but he dealt in plain and startling facts that roused his hearers from their careless indifference. He supported his statements and theories by Scripture proof as he progressed. A convincing power attended his words that seemed to stamp them as the language of truth.

He was courteous and sympathetic. When every seat in the house was full, and the platform and places about the pulpit seemed overcrowded, I have seen him leave the desk, and walk down the aisle, and take some feeble old man or

MILLER PREACHING IN THE GREAT TENT.

woman by the hand and find a seat for them, then return and resume his discourse. He was indeed rightly called "Father Miller," for he had a watchful care over those who came under his ministrations, was affectionate in his manner, of a genial disposition and tender heart.

He was an interesting speaker, and his exhortations, both to professed Christians and the impenitent, were appropriate and powerful. Sometimes a solemnity so marked as to be painful pervaded his meetings. A sense of the impending crisis of human events impressed the minds of the listening crowds. Many yielded to the conviction of the Spirit of God. Gray-haired men and aged women with trembling steps sought the anxious seats; those in the strength of maturity, the youth and children, were deeply stirred. Groans and the voice of weeping and of praise to God were mingled at the altar of prayer. [2]

Sinners inquired with weeping, "What must I do to be saved?" Those whose lives had been marked with dishonesty were anxious to make restitution. All who found peace in Christ longed to see others share the blessing. The hearts of parents were turned to their children, and the hearts of children to their parents. The barriers of pride and reserve were swept away. Heartfelt confessions were made, and the members of the household labored for the salvation of those who were nearest and dearest. Often was heard the sound of earnest intercession. Everywhere were souls in deep anguish, pleading with God. Many wrestled all night in prayer for the assurance that their own sins were pardoned, or for the conversion of their relatives or neighbors. That earnest, determined faith gained its object. Had the people of God continued to be thus importunate in prayer, pressing their petitions at the mercy seat, they would be in possession of a far richer experience than they now have. There is too little prayer, too little real conviction of sin; and the lack of living faith leaves many destitute of the grace so richly provided by our gracious Redeemer.

All classes flocked to the Adventist meetings. Rich and poor, high and low, were, from various causes, anxious to hear for themselves the doctrine of the Second Advent. The Lord held the spirit of opposition in check while His servants explained the reasons of their faith. Sometimes the instrument was feeble; but the Spirit of God gave power to His truth. The presence of holy angels was felt in these assemblies, and many were daily added to the believers. As the evidences of Christ's soon coming were repeated, vast crowds listened in breathless silence to the solemn words. Heaven and earth seemed to approach each other. The power of God would be felt upon old and young and middle-aged. Men sought their homes with praises upon their lips, and the glad sound rang out upon the still night air. None who attended those meetings can ever forget those scenes of deepest interest. [3]

Angels of God accompanied William Miller in his mission. He was firm and undaunted, fearlessly proclaiming the message committed to his trust. A world lying in wickedness and a cold, worldly church were enough to call into action all his energies and lead him willingly to endure toil, privation, and suffering. Although opposed by professed Christians and the world, and buffeted by Satan and his angels, he ceased not to preach the everlasting gospel to crowds wherever he was invited, sounding far and near the cry "Fear God, and give glory to him; for the hour of his judgment is come." [4]

---

[1] *Life Sketches*, pp. 20, 21.
[2] *Ibid.* pp. 26, 27.
[3] *The Spirit of Prophecy*, vol. 4, pp. 224, 225.
[4] *Early Writings*, p. 232.

CHAPTER SIX

Opposition Intensifies

The proclamation of a definite time for Christ's coming called forth great opposition from many of all classes, from the minister in the pulpit down to the most reckless, Heaven-daring sinner. "No man knoweth the day nor the hour!" was heard alike from the hypocritical minister and the bold scoffer. They closed their ears to the clear and harmonious explanation of the text by those who were pointing to the close of the prophetic periods and to the signs which Christ Himself had foretold as tokens of His advent.

Many who professed to love the Saviour declared that they had no opposition to the preaching of His coming; they merely objected to the definite time. God's all-seeing eye read their hearts. They did not wish to hear of Christ's coming to judge the world in righteousness. They had been unfaithful servants, their works would not bear the inspection of the heart-searching God, and they feared to meet their Lord. Like the Jews at the time of Christ's first advent, they were not prepared to welcome Jesus. Satan and his angels exulted and flung the taunt in the face of Christ and holy angels that His professed people had so little love for Him that they did not desire His appearing.

Unfaithful watchmen hindered the progress of the work of God. As the people were roused, and began to inquire the way of salvation, these leaders stepped in between them and the truth, seeking to quiet their fears by falsely interpreting the Word of God. In this work, Satan and unconsecrated ministers united, crying, Peace, peace, when God had not spoken peace. Like the Pharisees in Christ's day, many refused to enter the kingdom of Heaven themselves, and those who were entering in, they hindered. The blood of these souls will be required at their hand.

Wherever the message of truth was proclaimed, the most humble and devoted in the churches were the first to receive it. Those who studied the Bible for themselves could not but see the unscriptural character of the popular views of prophecy, and wherever the people were not deceived by the efforts of the clergy to misstate and pervert the faith, wherever they would search the Word of God for themselves, the Advent doctrine needed only to be compared with the Scriptures to establish its divine authority.

Many were persecuted by their unbelieving brethren. In order to retain their position in the church, some consented to be silent in regard to their hope; but others felt that loyalty to God forbade them thus to hide the truths which He had committed to their trust. Not a few were cut off from the fellowship of the church for no other reason than expressing their belief in the coming of Christ. Very precious to those who bore the trial of their faith were the words of the prophet, "Your brethren that hated you, that cast you out for my name's sake, said, Let the Lord be glorified: but he shall appear to your joy, and they shall be ashamed" (Isa. 66:5).

Angels of God were watching with the deepest interest the result of the warning. When the churches as a body rejected the message, angels turned away from them in sadness. Yet there were in the churches many who had not yet been tested in regard to the Advent truth. Many were deceived by husbands, wives, parents, or children, and were made to believe it a sin even to listen to such heresies as were taught by the Adventists. Angels were bidden to keep faithful watch over these souls; for another light was yet to shine upon them from the throne of God.*

---

* *The Spirit of Prophecy*, vol. 4, pp. 225-227.

CHAPTER SEVEN

A Time of Hope

The Adventists [in Portland, Maine] held meetings at this time in Beethoven Hall. [1]

With carefulness and trembling we approached the time when our Saviour was expected to appear. With solemn earnestness we sought, as a people, to purify our lives, that we might be ready to meet Him at His coming. Meetings were still held at private houses in different parts of the city, with the best results. Believers were encouraged to work for their friends and relatives, and conversions were multiplying day by day. Notwithstanding the opposition of ministers and churches, Beethoven Hall . . . was nightly crowded; especially was there a large congregation on Sundays. All classes flocked to these meetings. . . . Many came who, finding no room to stand, went away disappointed.

The order of the meetings was simple. A short and pointed discourse was usually given, then liberty was granted for general exhortation. There was, as a rule, the most perfect stillness possible for so large a crowd. [2]

Worldly business was for the most part laid aside for a few weeks. We carefully examined every thought and emotion of our hearts, as if upon our deathbeds, and in a few hours to close our eyes forever upon earthly scenes. There was no making of "ascension robes" for the great event; we felt the need of internal evidence that we were prepared to meet Christ, and our white robes were purity of soul, character cleansed from sin by the atoning blood of our Saviour.

But the time of expectation [in the spring of 1844] passed.

This was the first close test brought to bear upon those who believed and hoped that Jesus would come in the clouds of heaven. The disappointment of God's waiting people was great. The scoffers were triumphant, and won the weak and cowardly to their ranks. Some who had appeared to possess true faith seemed to have been influenced only by fear; and now their courage returned with the passing of the time, and they boldly united with the scoffers, declaring that they had never been duped to really believe the doctrine of Miller, who was a mad fanatic. Others, naturally yielding or vacillating, quietly deserted the cause.

We were perplexed and disappointed, yet did not renounce our faith. Many still clung to the hope that Jesus would not long delay His coming; the word of the Lord was sure, it could not fail. We felt that we had done our duty, we had lived up to our precious faith; we were disappointed, but not discouraged. The signs of the times denoted that the end of all things was at hand; we must watch and hold ourselves in readiness for the coming of the Master at any time. We must wait with hope and trust, not neglecting the assembling of ourselves together for instruction, encouragement, and comfort, that our light might shine forth into the darkness of the world. [3]

God designed to prove His people. His hand covered a mistake in the reckoning of the prophetic periods. Adventists did not discover the error, nor was it discovered by the most learned of their opponents. The latter said, "Your reckoning of the prophetic periods is correct. Some great event is about to take place; but it is not what Mr. Miller predicts; it is the conversion of the world, and not the second advent of Christ."

The time of expectation passed, and Christ did not appear for the deliverance of His people. Those who with sincere faith and love had looked for their Saviour experienced a bitter disappointment. Yet the Lord had accomplished His purpose: He had tested the hearts of those who professed to be waiting for His appearing. There were among them many who had been actuated by no higher motive than fear. Their profession of faith had not affected their hearts or their lives. When the expected event failed to take place, these persons declared that they were not disappointed; they had never believed that Christ would come. They were among the first to ridicule the sorrow of the true believers.

But Jesus and all the heavenly host looked with love and sympathy upon the tried and faithful yet disappointed ones. Could the vail separating the visible from the invisible world have been swept back, angels would have been seen drawing near to these steadfast souls, and shielding them from the shafts of Satan. [4]

---

[1] *Life Sketches,* p. 47.
[2] *Ibid.,* p. 54.
[3] *Ibid.,* pp. 56, 57.
[4] *The Spirit of Prophecy,* vol. 4, pp. 228, 229.

CHAPTER EIGHT

Leaving Babylon

When the churches spurned the counsel of God by rejecting the Advent message, the Lord rejected them. The first angel was followed by a second, proclaiming, "Babylon is fallen, is fallen, that great city, because she made all nations drink of the wine of the wrath of her fornication" (Rev. 14:8). This message was understood by Adventists to be an announcement of the moral fall of the churches in consequence of their rejection of the first message. The proclamation, "Babylon is fallen," was given in the summer of 1844, and as the result, about fifty thousand withdrew from these churches.

The term Babylon, derived from Babel, and signifying confusion, is applied in Scripture to the various forms of false or apostate religion. But the message announcing the fall of Babylon must apply to some religious body that was once pure, and has become corrupt. It cannot be the Romish Church which is here meant; for that church has been in a fallen condition for many centuries. But how appropriate the figure as applied to the Protestant churches, all professing to derive their doctrines from the Bible, yet divided into almost innumerable sects. The unity for which Christ prayed does not exist. Instead of one Lord, one faith, one baptism, there are numberless conflicting creeds and theories. Religious faith appears so confused and discordant that the world know not what to believe as truth. God is not in all this; it is the work of man—the work of Satan.

In Revelation 17, Babylon is represented as a woman, a figure which is used in the Scriptures as the symbol of a church. A virtuous woman represents a pure church, a vile woman an apostate church. Babylon is said to be a harlot;

and the prophet beheld her drunken with the blood of saints and martyrs. The Babylon thus described represents Rome, that apostate church which has so cruelly persecuted the followers of Christ. But Babylon the harlot is the mother of daughters who follow her example of corruption. Thus are represented those churches that cling to the doctrines and traditions of Rome and follow her worldly practices, and whose fall is announced in the second angel's message. . . .

The great sin charged against Babylon is that she "made all nations drink of the wine of the wrath of her fornication." This cup of intoxication which she presents to the world represents the false doctrines which she has accepted as a result of her unlawful connection with the great ones of the earth. Friendship with the world corrupts her faith, and in her turn she exerts a corrupting influence upon the world by teaching doctrines which are apposed to the plainest statements of the Word of God.

Prominent among these false doctrines is that of the temporal millennium—a thousand years of spiritual peace and prosperity, in which the world is to be converted, before the coming of Christ. This siren song has lulled thousands of souls to sleep over the abyss of eternal ruin.

The doctrine of the natural immortality of the soul has opened the way for the artful working of Satan through modern Spiritualism; and besides the Romish errors, purgatory, prayers for the dead, invocation of saints, etc., which have sprung from this source, it has led many Protestants to deny the resurrection and the judgment, and has given rise to the revolting heresy of eternal torment, and the dangerous delusion of Universalism.

And even more dangerous and more widely held than these are the assumptions that the law of God was abolished at the cross, and that the first day of the week is now a holy day, instead of the Sabbath of the fourth commandment.

When faithful teachers expound the Word of God, there arise men of learning, ministers professing to understand the Scriptures, who denounce sound doctrine as heresy, and thus turn away inquirers after truth. Were it not that the world is hopelessly intoxicated with the wine of Babylon, multitudes would be convicted and converted by the plain, cutting truths of the Word of God. The sin of the world's impenitence lies at the door of the church.

God sent His professed people a message that would have corrected the evils which separated them from His favor. A state of union, faith, and love had been produced among those who from every denomination in Christendom received the Advent doctrine; and had the churches in general accepted the same truth, the same blessed results would have followed. But Babylon scornfully rejected the last means which Heaven had in reserve for her restoration, and then, with greater eagerness, she turned to seek the friendship of the world.

Those who preached the first message had no purpose or expectation of causing divisions in the churches, or of forming separate organizations. "In all my labors," said William Miller, "I never had the desire or thought to establish any separate interest from that of existing denominations, or to benefit one at the expense of another. I thought to benefit all. Supposing that all Christians would rejoice in the prospect of Christ's coming, and that those who could not see as I did would not love any the less those who should embrace this doctrine, I did not conceive there would ever be any necessity for separate meetings. My whole object was a desire to convert souls to God, to notify the world of a coming judgment, and to induce my fellowmen to make that preparation of heart which will enable them to meet their God in peace. The great majority of those who were converted under my labors united with the various existing churches. When individuals came to me to inquire respecting their duty, I always told them to go where they would feel at home; and I never favored any one denomination in my advice to such."

For a time many of the churches welcomed his labors; but as they decided against the Advent truth, they desired to suppress all agitation of the subject. Those who had accepted the doctrine were thus placed in a position of great trial and perplexity. They loved their churches, and were loath to separate from them; but as they were ridiculed and oppressed, denied the privilege of speaking of their hope, or of attending preaching upon the Lord's coming, many at last arose and cast off the yoke which had been imposed upon them. . . .

Adventists, seeing that the churches rejected the testimony of God's Word, could no longer regard them as constituting the church of Christ, "the pillar and ground of the truth"; and as the message, "Babylon is fallen," began to be proclaimed, they felt themselves justified in separating from their former connection. . . .

At the proclamation of the first angel's message, the people of God were in Babylon; and many true Christians are still to be found in her communion. Not a few who have never seen the special truths for this time are dissatisfied with their present position, and are longing for clearer light. They look in vain for the image of Christ in the church. As the churches depart more and more widely from the truth, and ally themselves more closely with the world, the time will come when those who fear and honor God can no longer remain in connection with them. Those that "believed not the truth, but had pleasure in unrighteousness" will be left to receive "strong delusion," and to "believe a lie" (2 Thess. 2:11, 12). Then the spirit of persecution will again be revealed. But the light of truth will shine upon all whose hearts are open to receive it, and all the children of the Lord still in Babylon will heed the call, "Come out of her, my people." *

---

* *The Spirit of Prophecy*, vol. 4, pp. 232-240.

CHAPTER NINE

The Tarrying Time

When the year 1843 entirely passed away unmarked by the advent of Jesus, those who had looked in faith for His appearing were for a time left in doubt and perplexity. But notwithstanding their disappointment, many continued to search the Scriptures, examining anew the evidences of their faith, and carefully studying the prophecies to obtain further light. The Bible testimony in support of their position seemed clear and conclusive. Signs which could not be mistaken pointed to the coming of Christ as near. The believers could not explain their disappointment; yet they felt assured that God had led them in their past experience.

Their faith was greatly strengthened by the direct and forcible application of those scriptures which set forth a tarrying time. As early as 1842, the Spirit of God had moved upon Charles Fitch to devise the prophetic chart, which was generally regarded by Adventists as a fulfillment of the command given by the prophet Habakkuk, "to write the vision and make it plain upon tables." No one, however, then saw the tarrying time, which was brought to view in the same prophecy. After the disappointment, the full meaning of this scripture became apparent. Thus speaks the prophet: "Write the vision, and make it plain upon tables, that he may run that readeth it. For the vision is yet for an appointed time, but at the end it shall speak, and not lie: though it tarry, wait for it; because it will surely come, it will not tarry" (Hab. 2:2, 3).

A portion of Ezekiel's prophecy also was a source of much strength and comfort to believers: "And the word of the Lord came unto me, saying, Son of man, what is that

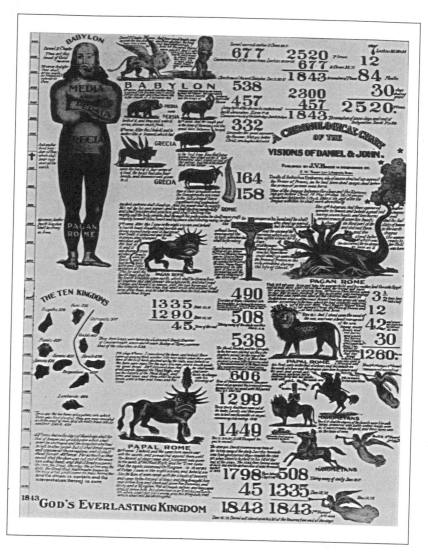

1844 CHART

proverb that ye have in the land of Israel, saying, The days are prolonged, and every vision faileth? Tell them therefore, Thus saith the Lord God, . . . The days are at hand, and the effect of every vision. . . . I will speak, and the word that I shall speak shall come to pass; it shall be no more prolonged. . . . They of the house of Israel say, The vision that he seeth is for many days to come, and he prophesieth of the times that are far off. Therefore say unto them, Thus saith the Lord God; There shall none of my words be prolonged any more, but the word which I have spoken shall be done" (Eze. 12:21-28).

The waiting ones rejoiced that He who knows the end from the beginning had looked down through the ages, and, foreseeing their disappointment, had given them words of courage and hope. Had it not been for such portions of Scripture, showing that they were in the right path, their faith would have failed in that trying hour.

In the parable of the ten virgins, Matthew 25, the experience of Adventists is illustrated by the incidents of an Eastern marriage. "Then shall the kingdom of heaven be likened unto ten virgins, which took their lamps, and went forth to meet the bridegroom." "While the bridegroom tarried, they all slumbered and slept." The widespread movement under the proclamation of the first message answered to the going forth of the virgins, while the passing of the time of expectation, the disappointment, and the delay were represented by the tarrying of the bridegroom. After the definite time had passed [the first time], the true believers were still united in the belief that the end of all things was at hand; but it soon became evident that they were losing, to some extent, their zeal and devotion, and were falling into the state denoted in the parable by the slumbering of the virgins during the tarrying time. [1]

Our hopes now centered on the coming of the Lord in 1844. . . .

DISAPPOINTED

How tedious and lonesome the hours,
　　While Jesus, my Saviour, delays!
I have sought Him in solitude's bowers,
　　And looked for Him all the long days.

Yet He lingers—I pray tell me why
　　His chariot no sooner returns?
To see Him in clouds of the sky,
　　My soul with intensity burns.

I long to be with Him at home,
　　My heart swallowed up in His love,
On the fields of New Eden to roam,
　　And to dwell with my Saviour above.
　　　　　　　　　　　—William Miller

    This was the happiest year of my life. My heart was full of glad expectation; but I felt great pity and anxiety for those who were in discouragement and had no hope in Jesus. We united, as a people, in earnest prayer for a true experience and the unmistakable evidence of our acceptance with God.

    We needed great patience, for the scoffers were many. We were frequently greeted by scornful references to our former disappointment. The orthodox churches used every means to prevent the belief in Christ's soon coming from spreading. No liberty was granted in their meetings to those who dared mention a hope of the soon coming of Christ. Professed lovers of Jesus scornfully rejected the tidings that He whom they claimed as their best Friend was soon to visit them. They were excited and angered against those who proclaimed the news of His coming, and who rejoiced that they should speedily behold Him in His glory. [2]

[1] *The Spirit of Prophecy,* vol. 4, pp. 241-243.
[2] *Life Sketches,* pp. 59, 60.

CHAPTER TEN

A Fanatical Few

About this time, fanaticism began to appear. Some who professed to be zealous believers in the message rejected the Word of God as the one infallible guide, and, claiming to be led by the Spirit, gave themselves up to the control of their own feelings, impressions, and imaginations. There were some who manifested a blind and bigoted zeal, denouncing all who would not sanction their course. Their fanatical ideas and exercises met with no sympathy from the great body of Adventists; yet they served to bring reproach upon the cause of truth.

Satan was seeking by this means to oppose and destroy the work of God. The people had been greatly stirred by the Advent movement, thousands of sinners had been converted, and faithful men were giving themselves to the work of proclaiming the truth, even in the tarrying time. The prince of evil was losing his subjects; and in order to bring reproach upon the cause of God, he sought to deceive those who professed the faith, and to drive them to extremes. Then his agents stood ready to seize upon every error, every failure, every unbecoming act, and hold it up before the people in the most exaggerated light, to render Adventists and their faith odious. Thus the greater the number whom he could crowd in to make a profession of the Advent faith while his power controlled their hearts, the greater advantage would he gain by calling attention to them as representatives of the whole body of believers. . . .

Satan contests every inch of ground over which God's people advance in their journey toward the heavenly city. In all the history of the church, no reformation has been carried forward without encountering serious obstacles. . . .

William Miller had no sympathy with those influences that led to fanaticism. He declared . . . that every spirit should be tested by the Word of God: "The devil has great power over the minds of some at the present day. And how shall we know what manner of spirit they are of? The Bible answers: 'By their fruits ye shall know them.' " "There are many spirits gone out into the world; and we are commanded to try the spirits. The spirit that does not cause us to live soberly, righteously, and godly in this present world is not the spirit of Christ. I am more and more convinced that Satan has much to do in these wild movements." "Many among us, who pretend to be wholly sanctified, are following the traditions of men, and apparently are as ignorant of truth as others who make no such pretensions, and are not half so modest."

"The spirit of error will lead us from the truth; and the Spirit of God will lead us into truth. But, say you, a man may be in error, and think he has the truth. What then? We answer, The Spirit and Word agree. If a man judges himself by the Word of God, and finds a perfect harmony through the whole Word, then he must believe he has the truth; but if he finds the spirit by which he is led does not harmonize with the whole tenor of God's law or book, then let him walk carefully, lest he be caught in the snare of the devil." "I have often obtained more evidence of inward piety from a kindling eye, a wet cheek, and a choked utterance, than from all the noise in Christendom.". . .

The fact that a few fanatics worked their way into the ranks of Adventists is no more a reason to decide that the movement was not of God, than is the presence of fanatics and deceivers in the church in Paul's or Luther's day a sufficient excuse for discarding or ridiculing their work. Let the people of God arouse out of sleep, and begin in earnest the work of repentance and reformation, let them search the

Scriptures to learn the truth as it is in Jesus, let them make an entire consecration to God, and evidence will not be wanting that Satan is still active and vigilant. With all possible deception will he manifest his power, calling to his aid all the fallen angels of his realm.

It was not the proclamation of the Advent message that created fanaticism and division. These appeared in the summer of 1844, when Adventists were in a state of doubt and perplexity concerning their real position. The preaching of the first message in 1843, and of the midnight cry in 1844, tended directly to repress fanaticism and dissension. Those who participated in these solemn movements were in harmony; their hearts were filled with love for one another, and for Jesus, whom they expected soon to see. The one faith, the one blessed hope, lifted them above the control of any human influence, and proved a shield against the assaults of Satan.

"While the bridegroom tarried, they all slumbered and slept. And at midnight there was a cry made, Behold, the bridegroom cometh; go ye out to meet him. Then all those virgins arose, and trimmed their lamps" (Matt. 25:5-7).*

---

* *The Spirit of Prophecy*, vol. 4, pp. 243-248.

CHAPTER ELEVEN

"Behold, the Bridegroom Cometh"

In the summer of 1844, Adventists discovered the mistake in their former reckoning of the prophetic periods, and settled upon the correct position. The 2300 days of Daniel 8:14, which all believed to extend to the second coming of Christ, had been thought to end in the spring of 1844; but it was now seen that this period extended to the autumn of the same year, and the minds of Adventists were fixed upon this point as the time for the Lord's appearing. The proclamation of this time message was another step in the fulfillment of the parable of the marriage, whose application to the experience of Adventists had already been clearly seen. As in the parable the cry was raised at midnight announcing the approach of the bridegroom, so in the fulfillment, midway between the spring of 1844, when it was first supposed that the 2300 days would close, and the autumn of 1844, at which time it was afterward found that they were really to close, such a cry was raised, in the very words of Scripture: "Behold, the bridegroom cometh; go ye out to meet him."

Like a tidal wave the movement swept over the land. From city to city, from village to village, and into remote country places it went, until the waiting people of God were fully aroused. Before this proclamation, fanaticism disappeared, like early frost before the rising sun. Believers once more found their position, and hope and courage animated their hearts.

The work was free from those extremes which are ever

manifested when there is human excitement without the controlling influence of the Word and Spirit of God. It was similar in character to those seasons of humiliation and returning unto the Lord which among ancient Israel followed messages of reproof from His servants. It bore the characteristics which mark the work of God in every age. There was little ecstatic joy, but rather deep searching of heart, confession of sin, and forsaking of the world. A preparation to meet the Lord was the burden of agonizing spirits. There was persevering prayer, and unreserved consecration to God.

Said William Miller, in describing that work: "There is no great expression of joy; that is, as it were, suppressed for a future occasion, when all heaven and earth will rejoice together with joy unspeakable and full of glory. There is no shouting; that, too, is reserved for the shout from heaven. The singers are silent; they are waiting to join the angelic hosts, the choir from heaven. No arguments are used or needed; all seem convinced that they have the truth. There is no clashing of sentiments; all are of one heart and of one mind."

VIEW OF FATHER MILLER'S TENT AND CAMP GROUND
AT NEWARK.

Of all the great religious movements since the days of the apostles, none have been more free from human imperfection and the wiles of Satan than was that of the autumn of 1844. Even now, after the lapse of forty years [written in 1884], all who shared in that movement and who have stood firm upon the platform of truth still feel the holy influence of that blessed work, and bear witness that it was of God.

At the call "The bridegroom cometh; go ye out to meet him," the waiting ones "arose and trimmed their lamps"; they studied the Word of God with an intensity of interest before unknown. Angels were sent from Heaven to arouse those who had become discouraged, and prepare them to receive the message. The work did not stand in the wisdom and learning of men, but in the power of God. It was not the most talented, but the most humble and devoted, who were the first to hear and obey the call. Farmers left their crops standing in the fields, mechanics laid down their tools, and with tears and rejoicing went out to give the warning. Those who had formerly led in the cause were among the last to join in this movement. The churches in general closed their doors against it, and a large company who had the living testimony withdrew from their connection. In the providence of God, this cry united with the second angel's message, and gave power to that work.

The midnight cry was not so much carried by argument, though the Scripture proof was clear and conclusive. There went with it an impelling power that moved the soul. There was no doubt, no questioning. Upon the occasion of Christ's triumphal entry into Jerusalem, the people who were assembled from all parts of the land to keep the feast, flocked to the Mount of Olives, and as they joined the throng that were escorting Jesus, they caught the inspiration of the hour, and helped to swell the shout "Blessed is he that cometh in the name of the Lord!" (Matt. 21:9). In like manner did unbelievers who flocked to the Adventist meetings—some from curiosity, some merely to ridicule—feel the convincing power attending the message, "Behold, the bridegroom cometh!"

At that time there was faith that brought answers to prayer—faith that had respect to the recompense of reward. Like showers of rain upon the thirsty earth, the Spirit of grace descended upon the earnest seekers. Those who expected soon to stand face-to-face with their Redeemer felt a solemn joy that was unutterable. The softening, subduing power of the Holy Spirit melted the heart, as wave after wave of the glory of God swept over the faithful, believing ones. [1]

With diligent searching of heart and humble confessions, we came prayerfully up to the time of expectation. Every morning we felt that it was our first work to secure the evidence that our lives were right before God. We realized that if we were not advancing in holiness, we were sure to retrograde. Our interest for one another increased; we prayed much with and for one another. We assembled in the orchards and groves to commune with God and to offer up our petitions to Him, feeling more fully in His presence when surrounded by His natural works. The joys of salvation were more necessary to us than our food and drink. If clouds obscured our minds, we dared not rest or sleep till they were swept away by the consciousness of our acceptance with the Lord.

The waiting people of God approached the hour when they fondly hoped their joys would be complete in the coming of the Saviour. But the time again passed unmarked by the advent of Jesus. It was a bitter disappointment that fell upon the little flock whose faith had been so strong and whose hope had been so high. But we were surprised that we felt so free in the Lord, and were so strongly sustained by His strength and grace. [2]

---

[1] *The Spirit of Prophecy,* vol. 4, pp. 248-251.
[2] *Life Sketches,* pp. 60, 61.

CHAPTER TWELVE

A Terrible Disappointment

A feeling of awe, a fear that the message might be true, had for a time served as a restraint upon the unbelieving world. After the passing of the time, this did not at once disappear; they dared not triumph over the disappointed ones; but as no tokens of God's wrath were seen, they recovered from their fears, and resumed their reproach and ridicule. A large class who had professed to believe in the Lord's soon coming renounced their faith. Some who had been very confident were so deeply wounded in their pride that they felt like fleeing from the world. Like Jonah, they complained of God, and chose death rather than life. Those who had based their faith upon the opinions of others, and not upon the word of God, were now as ready to again exchange their views. The scoffers won the weak and cowardly to their ranks, and all united in declaring that there could be no more fears or expectations now. The time had passed, the Lord had not come, and the world might remain the same for thousands of years.

The earnest, sincere believers had given up all for Christ, and had shared His presence as never before. They had, as they believed, given their last warning to the world, and, expecting soon to be received into the society of their divine Master and the heavenly angels, they had, to a great extent, withdrawn from the unbelieving multitude. With intense desire they had prayed, "Come, Lord Jesus, and come quickly." But He had not come. And now to take up again the heavy burden of life's cares and perplexities, and to endure the taunts and sneers of a scoffing world, was indeed a terrible trial of faith and patience. [1]

Jesus did not come to the earth as the waiting, joyful company expected, to cleanse the sanctuary by purifying the earth by fire. I saw that they were correct in their reckoning of the prophetic periods; prophetic time closed in 1844, and Jesus entered the most holy place to cleanse the sanctuary at the ending of the days. Their mistake consisted in not understanding what the sanctuary was and the nature of its cleansing. As I looked again at the waiting, disappointed company, they appeared sad. They carefully examined the evidences of their faith and followed down through the reckoning of the prophetic periods, but could discover no mistake. The time had been fulfilled, but where was their Saviour? They had lost Him. [2]

"Our fondest hopes and expectations were blasted, and such a spirit of weeping came over us as I never experienced before. It seemed that the loss of all earthly possessions could have been no comparison. We wept, and wept, until the day dawn." — Hiram Edson.

"The disappointment . . . was a bitter one. . . . When Elder Himes visited Portland, Me., a few days after the passing of the time, and stated that the brethren should prepare for another cold winter, my feelings were almost uncontrollable. I left the place of meeting and wept like a child." — James White.

"It passed, and the next day it seemed as though all demons from the bottomless pit were let loose upon us. The same ones and many more who were crying for mercy two days before, were now mixed with the rabble and mocking, scoffing, and threatening in a most blasphemous manner." — William Miller.

"The day passed, and another twenty-four hours followed, but deliverance did not come. Hope sunk and courage died within them. . . . The effect of this disappointment can be realized only by those who experienced it." — Joseph Bates.

We were disappointed, but not disheartened. We resolved to refrain from murmuring at the trying ordeal by which the Lord was purging us from the dross and refining us like gold in the furnace; to submit patiently to the process of purifying that God deemed needful for us; and to wait with patient hope for the Saviour to redeem His tried and faithful ones. [3]

Yet this disappointment was not so great as was that experienced by the disciples at the time of Christ's first advent. When Jesus rode triumphantly into Jerusalem, His followers believed that He was about to ascend the throne of David, and deliver Israel from her oppressors. With high hopes and joyful anticipations they vied with one another in showing honor to their King. Many spread their outer garments as a carpet in His path, or strewed before Him the leafy branches of the palm. In their enthusiastic joy they united in the glad acclaim, "Hosanna to the Son of David!" When the Pharisees, disturbed and angered by this outburst of rejoicing, wished Jesus to rebuke His disciples, He replied, "If these should hold their peace, the stones would immediately cry out" (Luke 19:40).

Prophecy must be fulfilled. The disciples were accomplishing the purpose of God; yet they were doomed to a bitter disappointment. But a few days had passed ere they witnessed the Saviour's agonizing death, and laid Him in the tomb. Their expectations had not been realized in a single particular, and their hopes died with Jesus. Not till their Lord had come forth triumphant from the grave could they perceive that all had been foretold by prophecy, and "that Christ must needs have suffered, and risen again from the dead" (Acts 17:3). In like manner was prophecy fulfilled in the first and second angels' messages. They were given at the right time, and accomplished the work which God designed to accomplish by them.

The world had been looking on, expecting that if the time passed and Christ did not appear, the whole system of Adventism would be given up. But while many, under strong temptation, yielded their faith, there were some who stood firm. They could detect no error in their reckoning of the prophetic periods. The ablest of their opponents had not succeeded in overthrowing their position. True, there had been a failure as to the expected event, but even this could not shake their faith in the Word of God. When Jonah proclaimed in the streets of Nineveh that within forty days the city would be overthrown, the Lord accepted the humiliation of the Ninevites, and extended their period of probation; yet the message of Jonah was sent of God, and Nineveh was tested according to His will. Adventists believed that God had in like manner led them to warn the world of the coming judgment, and notwithstanding their disappointment, they felt assured that they had reached a most important crisis.

The parable of the wicked servant was regarded as applying to those who desired to put off the coming of the Lord: "If that evil servant shall say in his heart, My lord delayeth his coming; and shall begin to smite his fellowservants, and to eat and drink with the drunken; the lord of that servant shall come in a day when he looketh not for him, and in an hour that he is not aware of, and shall cut him asunder, and appoint him his portion with the hypocrites" (Matt. 24:48-51).

The feelings of those who held fast the Advent truth are expressed in the words of William Miller: "Were I to live my life over again, with the same evidence that I then had, to be honest with God and men I should have to do as I have done." "I hope I have cleansed my garments from the blood of souls; I feel that, as far as possible, I have freed myself from all guilt in their condemnation." "Although I have been twice disappointed," wrote this man of God, "I am not yet cast down or discouraged." "My hope in the coming of Christ is as strong as ever. I have done only what, after years of sober consideration, I felt it my solemn duty to do. If I have erred, it has been on the side of charity, the love of my fellowman, and my conviction of duty to God."

"One thing I do know, I have preached nothing but what I believed; and God's hand has been with me, His power has been manifested in the work, and much good has been effected." "Many thousands, to all human appearance, have been made to study the Scriptures by the preaching of the time; and by that means, through faith and the sprinkling of the blood of Christ, have been reconciled to God." "I have never courted the smiles of the proud, nor quailed when the world frowned. I shall not now purchase their favor, nor shall I go beyond duty to tempt their hate. I shall never seek my life at their hands, nor shrink, I hope, from losing it, if God in His good providence so orders."

"I have fixed my mind upon another time, and here I mean to stand until God gives me more light—And that is *Today, TODAY,* and *TODAY,* until He comes."—William Miller.

God did not forsake His people; His Spirit still abode with those who did not rashly deny the light which they had received, and denounce the Advent movement. The apostle Paul, looking down through the ages, had written words of encouragement and warning for the tried, waiting ones at this crisis: "Cast not away therefore your confidence, which hath great recompense of reward. For ye have need of patience, that, after ye have done the will of God, ye might receive the promise. For yet a little while, and he that shall come will come, and will not tarry. Now the just shall live by faith: but if any man draw back, my soul shall have no pleasure in him.

But we are not of them who draw back unto perdition; but of them that believe to the saving of the soul" (Heb. 10:35-39).

The people here addressed were in danger of making shipwreck of faith. They had done the will of God in following the guidance of His Spirit and His Word; yet they could not understand His purpose in their past experience, nor could they discern the pathway before them, and they were tempted to doubt whether God had indeed been leading them. At this time the words were specially applicable, "Now the just shall live by faith."

As the bright light of the midnight cry had shone upon their pathway, and they had seen the prophecies unsealed, and the rapidly fulfilling signs telling that the coming of Christ was near, Adventists had walked, as it were, by sight. But now, bowed down by disappointed hopes, they could stand only by faith in God and in His Word. The scoffing world were saying, "You have been deceived. Give up your faith, and say that the Advent movement was of Satan." But God's Word declared, "If any man draw back, My soul shall have no pleasure in him." To renounce their faith now, and deny the power of the Holy Spirit which had attended the message, would be drawing back toward perdition.

They were encouraged to steadfastness by the words of Paul, "Cast not away therefore your confidence"; "ye have need of patience"; "for yet a little while, and he that shall come will come, and will not tarry." Their only safe course was to cherish the light which they had already received of God, hold fast to His promises, and continue to search the Scriptures, and patiently wait and watch to receive further light. [4]

---

[1] *The Spirit of Prophecy,* vol. 4, pp. 252, 253.
[2] *Early Writings,* pp. 243, 244.
[3] *Life Sketches,* pp. 61, 62.
[4] *The Spirit of Prophecy,* vol. 4, pp. 253-257.

CHAPTER THIRTEEN

The Tired Warrior

After the great disappointment in 1844, Satan and his angels were busily engaged in laying snares to unsettle the faith of the body. He affected the minds of persons who had had an experience in the messages, and who had an appearance of humility. Some pointed to the future for the fulfillment of the first and second messages, while others pointed far back into the past, declaring that they had been there fulfilled. These were gaining an influence over the minds of the inexperienced and unsettling their faith. Some were searching the Bible to build up a faith of their own, independent of the body. Satan exulted in all this; for he knew that those who broke loose from the anchor he could affect by different errors and drive about with divers winds of doctrine. Many who had led in the first and second messages now denied them, and there was division and confusion throughout the body.

My attention was then called to William Miller. He looked perplexed and was bowed with anxiety and distress for his people. The company who had been united and loving in 1844 were losing their love, opposing one another, and falling into a cold, backslidden state. As he beheld this, grief wasted his strength. I saw leading men watching him, and fearing lest he should receive the third angel's message and the commandments of God. And as he would lean toward the light from heaven, these men would lay some plan to draw his mind away. A human influence was exerted to keep him in darkness and to retain his influence among those who opposed the truth.

At length William Miller raised his voice against the light

from heaven. He failed in not receiving the message which would have fully explained his disappointment and cast a light and glory on the past, which would have revived his exhausted energies, brightened his hope, and led him to glorify God. He leaned to human wisdom instead of divine, but being broken with arduous labor in his Master's cause and by age, he was not as accountable as those who kept him from the truth. They are responsible; the sin rests upon them.

If William Miller could have seen the light of the third message, many things which looked dark and mysterious to him would have been explained. But his brethren professed so deep love and interest for him that he thought he could not tear away from them. His heart would incline toward the truth, and then he looked at his brethren; they opposed it. Could he tear away from those who had stood side by side with him in proclaiming the coming of Jesus? He thought they surely would not lead him astray.

THE CHAPEL AND GROVE WHERE MR. MILLER
RECEIVED THE CALL TO PREACH.

God suffered him to fall under the power of Satan, the dominion of death, and hid him in the grave from those who were constantly drawing him from the truth. Moses erred as he was about to enter the Promised Land. So also, I saw that William Miller erred as he was soon to enter the heavenly Canaan, in suffering his influence to go against the truth. Others led him to this; others must account for it. But angels watch the precious dust of this servant of God, and he will come forth at the sound of the last trump.*

* *Early Writings*, pp. 256-258.

THE RESTING PLACE OF WILLIAM AND LUCY P. MILLER

CHAPTER FOURTEEN

Searching for Answers

The scripture which above all others had been both the foundation and central pillar of the Advent faith was the declaration "Unto two thousand and three hundred days; then shall the sanctuary be cleansed" (Dan. 8:14). These had been familiar words to all believers in the Lord's soon coming. By the lips of thousands was this prophecy joyfully repeated as the watchword of their faith. All felt that upon the events therein brought to view depended their brightest expectations and most cherished hopes. These prophetic days had been shown to terminate in the autumn of 1844. In common with the rest of the Christian world, Adventists then held that the earth, or some portion of it, was the sanctuary, and that the cleansing of the sanctuary was the purification of the earth by the fires of the last great day. This they understood would take place at the second coming of Christ. Hence the conclusion that Christ would return to the earth in 1844.

But the appointed time came, and the Lord did not appear. The believers knew that God's Word could not fail; their interpretation of the prophecy must be at fault; but where was the mistake? Many rashly cut the knot of difficulty by denying that the 2300 days ended in 1844. No reason could be given for this position, except that Christ had not come at the time of expectation. They argued that if the prophetic days had ended in 1844, Christ would then have come to cleanse the sanctuary by the purification of the earth by fire; and that since He had not come, the days could not have ended.

To accept this conclusion was to renounce the former

reckoning of the prophetic periods, and involve the whole question in confusion. It was a deliberate surrender of positions which had been reached through earnest, prayerful study of the Scriptures, by minds enlightened by the Spirit of God, and hearts burning with its living power; positions which had withstood the most searching criticism and the most bitter opposition of popular religionists and worldly-wise men, and which had stood firm against the combined forces of learning and eloquence, and the taunts and revilings alike of the honorable and the base. And all this sacrifice was made in order to maintain the theory that the earth is the sanctuary.

God had led His people in the great Advent movement; His power and glory had attended the work, and He would not permit it to end in darkness and disappointment, to be reproached as a false and fanatical excitement. He would not leave His Word involved in doubt and uncertainty. Though the majority of Adventists abandoned their former reckoning of the prophetic periods, and consequently denied the correctness of the movement based thereon, a few were unwilling to renounce points of faith and experience that were sustained by the Scriptures and by the special witness of the Spirit of God. They believed that they had adopted sound principles of interpretation in their study of the Scriptures, and that it was their duty to hold fast the truths already gained, and to still pursue the same course of biblical research. With earnest prayer they reviewed their position, and studied the Scriptures to discover their mistake. As they could see no error in their explanation of the prophetic periods, they were led to examine more closely the subject of the sanctuary.*

---

* *The Spirit of Prophecy,* vol. 4, pp. 258-260.

CHAPTER FIFTEEN

A Deeper Understanding

At the termination of the 2300 days, in 1844, no sanctuary had existed on earth for many centuries; therefore the sanctuary in heaven must be the one brought to view in the declaration "Unto two thousand and three hundred days; then shall the sanctuary be cleansed." But how could a sanctuary in heaven need cleansing? Turning again to the Scriptures, the students of prophecy learned that the cleansing was not a removal of physical impurities, for it was to be accomplished with blood, and therefore must be a cleansing from sin. Thus says the apostle: "It was therefore necessary that the patterns of things in the heavens should be purified with these [the blood of animals]; but the heavenly things themselves with better sacrifices than these [even the precious blood of Christ]" (Heb. 9:23). To obtain a further knowledge of the cleansing to which the prophecy points, it was necessary to understand the ministration of the heavenly sanctuary. This could be learned only from the ministration of the earthly sanctuary; for Paul declares that the priests who officiated there served "unto the example and shadow of heavenly things" (Heb. 8:5).

The ministration of the earthly sanctuary consisted of two divisions: the priests ministered daily in the holy place, while once a year the high priest performed a special work of atonement in the Most Holy, for the cleansing of the sanctuary. Day by day the repentant sinner brought his offering to the door of the tabernacle, and, placing his hand upon the victim's head, confessed his sins, thus in figure transferring them to the innocent sacrifice. The animal was then slain, and the blood or the flesh was carried by the priest into the holy place. Thus the sin was, in figure, transferred to the sanctuary. Such was the work that went forward throughout the year. The continual transfer of sins to the sanctuary rendered a further work of ministration necessary in order for their removal. On the tenth day of the seventh month the high priest entered the inner apartment, or most holy place, which he was forbidden, on pain of death, to enter at any other time. The cleansing of the sanctuary then performed completed the yearly round of service.

On the great day of atonement, two kids of the goats were brought to the door of the tabernacle, and lots were cast upon them, "one lot for the Lord, and the other lot for the

ON THE DAY OF ATONEMENT

scape-goat" (Lev. 16:8). The goat upon which fell the lot for the Lord was to be slain as a sin-offering for the people. And the priest was to bring his blood within the vail, and sprinkle it upon the mercy seat, and before the mercy seat. "And he shall make an atonement for the holy place, because of the uncleanness of the children of Israel, and because of their transgressions in all their sins; and so shall he do for the tabernacle of the congregation, that remaineth among them in the midst of their uncleanness" (verse 16).

"And Aaron shall lay both his hands upon the head of the live goat, and confess over him all the iniquities of the children of Israel, and all their transgressions in all their sins, putting them upon the head of the goat, and shall send him away by the hand of a fit man into the wilderness: and the goat shall bear upon him all their iniquities unto a land not inhabited" (verses 21, 22). The scape-goat came no more into the camp of Israel, and the man who led him away was required to wash himself and his clothing with water before returning to the camp.

The whole ceremony was designed to impress the Israelites with the holiness of God and His abhorrence of sin, and, further, to show them that they could not come in contact with sin without becoming polluted. Every man was required to afflict his soul while this work of atonement was going forward. All business was laid aside, and the whole congregation of Israel spent the day in solemn humiliation before God, with prayer, fasting, and deep searching of heart. . . .

Such was the service performed "unto the example and shadow of heavenly things." And what was done in type in the ministration of the earthly is done in reality in the ministration of the heavenly. After His ascension, our Saviour began His work as our high priest. Says Paul, "Christ is not entered into the holy places made with hands, which are the figures of the true; but into heaven itself, now to appear in the presence of God for us" (Heb. 9:24). In harmony with the typical service, He began His ministration in the holy place, and at the termination of the prophetic days in 1844, as foretold by Daniel the prophet, He entered the most holy to perform the last division of His solemn work—to cleanse the sanctuary.

As the sins of the people were anciently transferred, in figure, to the earthly sanctuary by the blood of the sin-offering, so our sins are, in fact, transferred to the heavenly sanctuary by the blood of Christ. And as the typical cleansing of the earthly was accomplished by the removal of the sins by which it had been polluted, so the actual cleansing of the heavenly is to be accomplished by the removal, or blotting out, of the sins which are there recorded. This necessitates an examination of the books of record to determine who, through repentance of sin and faith in christ, are entitled to the benefits of His atonement. The cleansing of the sanctuary therefore involves a work of investigative judgment. This work must be performed prior to the coming of Christ to redeem His people; for when He comes, His reward is with Him to give to every man according to his works (Rev. 22:12).

Thus those who followed in the advancing light of the prophetic Word saw that instead of coming to the earth at the termination of the 2300 days in 1844, Christ then entered the most holy place of the heavenly sanctuary, into the presence of God, to perform the closing work of atonement, preparatory to His coming.

It was seen, also, that while the sin-offering pointed to Christ as a sacrifice, and the high priest represented Christ as a mediator, the scape-goat typified Satan, the author of sin, upon whom the sins of the truly penitent will finally be placed. When the high priest, by virtue of the blood of the sin-offering, removed the sins from the sanctuary, he placed them upon the scape-goat. When Christ, by virtue of His own blood, removes the sins of His people from the heavenly sanctuary at the close of His ministration, He will place them upon Satan, who, in the execution of the judgment, must bear the final penalty. The scape-goat was sent away into a land not inhabited, never to come again into the congregation of Israel. So will Satan be forever banished from the presence of God and His people, and he will be blotted from existence in the final destruction of sin and sinners.*

* *The Spirit of Prophecy,* vol. 4, pp. 262-267.

CHAPTER SIXTEEN

The Mystery Solved

The subject of the sanctuary was the key which unlocked the mystery of the disappointment, showing that God had led His people in the great Advent movement. It opened to view a complete system of truth, connected and harmonious, and revealed present duty as it brought to light the position and work of God's people.

After the passing of the time of expectation, in 1844, Adventists still believed the Saviour's coming to be very near; they held that they had reached an important crisis, and that the work of Christ as man's intercessor before God, had ceased. Having given the warning of the judgment near, they felt that their work for the world was done, and they lost their burden of soul for the salvation of sinners, while the bold and blasphemous scoffing of the ungodly seemed to them another evidence that the Spirit of God had been withdrawn from the rejecters of His mercy. All this confirmed them in the belief that probation had ended, or, as they then expressed it, "the door of mercy was shut."

But clearer light came with the investigation of the sanctuary question. Now was seen the application of those words of Christ in the Revelation, addressed to the church at this very time: "These things saith he that is holy, he that is true, he that hath the key of David, he that openeth, and no man shutteth, and shutteth, and no man openeth; I know thy works: behold, I have set before thee an open door, and no man can shut it" (Rev. 3:7, 8). Here an open as well as a shut door is brought to view.

At the termination of the 2300 prophetic days in 1844, Christ changed His ministration from the holy to the most holy place. When, in the ministration of the earthly sanctuary, the high priest on the day of atonement entered the most holy place, the door of the holy place was closed, and the door of the most holy was opened. So when Christ passed from the holy to the most holy of the heavenly sanctuary, the door, or ministration, of the former apartment was closed, and the door, or ministration, of the latter was opened. Christ had ended one part of His work as our intercessor, to enter upon another portion of the work; and He still presented His blood before the Father in behalf of sinners. "Behold," He declares, "I have set before thee an open door, and no man can shut it." *

* *The Spirit of Prophecy,* vol. 4, pp. 268, 269.

CHAPTER SEVENTEEN

In the Most Holy Place

I was shown what did take place in heaven at the close of the prophetic periods in 1844. As Jesus ended His ministration in the holy place and closed the door of that apartment, a great darkness settled upon those who had heard and rejected the message of His coming, and they lost sight of Him. [1]

I saw a throne, and on it sat the Father and the Son. I gazed on Jesus' countenance and admired His lovely person. The Father's person I could not behold, for a cloud of glorious light covered Him. I asked Jesus if His Father had a form like Himself. He said He had, but I could not behold it, for, said He, "If you should once behold the glory of His person, you would cease to exist."

Before the throne I saw the Advent people—the church and the world. I saw two companies, one bowed down before the throne, deeply interested, while the other stood uninterested and careless. Those who were bowed before the throne would offer up their prayers and look to Jesus; then He would look to His Father, and appear to be pleading with Him. A light would come from the Father to the Son and from the Son to the praying company.

Then I saw an exceeding bright light come from the Father to the Son, and from the Son it waved over the people before the throne. But few would receive this great light. Many came out from under it and immediately resisted it; others were careless and did not cherish the light, and it moved off from them. Some cherished it, and went and bowed down with the little praying company. This company all received the light and rejoiced in it, and their countenances shone with its glory.

I saw the Father rise from the throne, and in a flaming chariot go into the holy of holies within the veil, and sit down. Then Jesus rose up from the throne, and the most of those who were bowed down arose with Him. I did not see one ray of light pass from Jesus to the careless multitude after He arose, and they were left in perfect darkness. Those who arose when Jesus did kept their eyes fixed on Him as He left the throne and led them out a little way. Then He raised His right arm, and we heard His lovely voice saying, "Wait here; I am going to My Father to receive the kingdom; keep your garments spotless, and in a little while I will return from the wedding and receive you to Myself."

Then a cloudy chariot, with wheels like flaming fire, surrounded by angels, came to where Jesus was. He stepped into the chariot and was borne to the holiest, where the Father sat. There I beheld Jesus, a great High Priest, standing before the Father. On the hem of His garment was a bell and a pomegranate, a bell and a pomegranate. Those who rose up with Jesus would send up their faith to Him in the holiest, and pray, "My Father, give us Thy Spirit." Then Jesus would breathe upon them the Holy Ghost. In that breath was light, power, and much love, joy, and peace.

I turned to look at the company who were still bowed before the throne; they did not know that Jesus had left it. Satan appeared to be by the throne, trying to carry on the work of God. I saw them look up to the throne and pray, "Father, give us Thy Spirit." Satan would then breathe upon them an unholy influence; in it there was light and much power, but no sweet love, joy, and peace. Satan's object was to keep them deceived and to draw back and deceive God's children. [2]

When Christ entered the most holy place of the heavenly

sanctuary to perform the closing work of the atonement, He committed to His servants the last message of mercy to be given to the world. Such is the warning of the third angel of Revelation 14. Immediately following its proclamation, the Son of man is seen by the prophet coming in glory to reap the harvest of the earth.

As foretold in the Scriptures, the ministration of Christ in the most holy place began at the termination of the prophetic days in 1844. To this time apply the words of the revelator, "The temple of God was opened in heaven, and there was seen in his temple the ark of his testament" (Rev. 11:19). The ark of God's testament is in the second apartment of the sanctuary. As Christ entered there, to minister in the sinner's behalf, the inner temple was opened, and the ark of God was brought to view. To those who by faith beheld the Saviour in His work of intercession, God's majesty and power were revealed. As the train of His glory filled the temple, light from the holy of holies was shed upon His waiting people on the earth.

They had by faith followed their High Priest from the holy to the most holy, and they saw Him pleading His blood before the ark of God. Within that sacred ark is the Father's law, the same that was spoken by god Himself amid the thunders of Sinai, and written with His own finger on the tables of stone. Not one command has been annulled; not a jot or tittle has been changed. While God gave to Moses a copy of His law, He preserved the great original in the sanctuary above. Tracing down its holy precepts, the seekers for truth found, in the very bosom of the Decalogue, the fourth commandment, as it was first proclaimed: "Remember the sabbath day, to keep it holy. Six days shalt thou labour, and do all thy work; but the seventh day is the sabbath of the Lord thy God: in it thou shalt not do any work, thou, nor thy son, nor thy daughter, thy manservant, nor thy maidservant, nor thy cattle, nor thy stranger that is within thy gates: for in six days the Lord made heaven and earth, the sea, and all that in them is, and rested the seventh day: wherefore the Lord blessed the Sabbath day, and hallowed it" (Ex. 20:8-11])

The Spirit of God impressed the hearts of these students of His Word. The conviction was urged upon them that they had ignorantly transgressed the fourth commandment by disregarding the Creator's rest-day. They began to examine the reasons for observing the first day of the week instead of the day which God had sanctified. They could find no evidence in the Scriptures that the fourth commandment had been abolished, or that the Sabbath had been changed; the blessing which first hallowed the seventh day had never been removed. They had been honestly seeking to know and do God's will, and now, as they saw themselves transgressors of His law, sorrow filled their hearts. They at once evinced their loyalty to God by keeping His Sabbath holy. [3]

With peculiar fitness may the Sabbath be called the foundation of many generations. Hallowed by the Creator's rest and blessing, it was kept by Adam in his innocence in holy Eden; by Adam, fallen yet repentant, when he was driven from his happy estate. It was kept by all the patriarchs, from Abel to righteous Noah, to Abraham, to Jacob. When the chosen people were in bondage in Egypt, many, in the midst of prevailing idolatry, lost their knowledge of God's law; but when the Lord delivered Israel, He proclaimed His law in awful grandeur to the assembled multitude, that they might know His will, and fear and obey Him forever.

From that day to the present, the knowledge of God's law has been preserved in the earth, and the Sabbath of the fourth commandment has been kept. Though the man of sin succeeded in trampling the Sabbath underfoot, yet even in the period of his supremacy there were, hidden in secret places, faithful souls who honored the Creator's rest-day.

Since the Reformation, there have been in every generation witnesses for God to uphold the standard of the ancient Sabbath. Though often in the midst of reproach and persecution, a constant testimony has been borne to this truth. Since 1844, in fulfillment of the prophecy of the third angel's message, the attention of the world has been called to the true Sabbath, and a constantly increasing number are returning to the observance of God's holy day. [4]

[1] *Early Writings,* p. 251.
[2] *Ibid.,* pp. 54-56
[3] *The Spirit of Prophecy,* vol. 4, pp. 273-275.
[4] *Ibid.,* pp. 285, 286.

CHAPTER EIGHTEEN

The Deliverance of God's People

It is at midnight that God manifests His power for the deliverance of His people. The sun appears, shining in its strength. Startling signs and wonders follow in quick succession. The wicked look with terror and amazement upon the scene, while the righteous behold with solemn joy the tokens of their deliverance. Everything in nature seems turned out of its course. The streams cease to flow. Dark, heavy clouds come up, and clash against each other. In the midst of the angry heavens is one clear space of indescribable glory, whence comes the voice of God like the sound of many waters, saying, "It is done."

That voice shakes the heavens and the earth. There is a mighty earthquake. The firmament appears to open and shut. The glory from the throne of God seems flashing through. The mountains shake like a reed in the wind, and ragged rocks are scattered on every side. There is a roar as of a coming tempest. The sea is lashed into fury. There is heard the shriek of the hurricane, like the voice of demons upon a mission of destruction.

The whole earth heaves and swells like the waves of the sea. Its surface is breaking up. Its very foundations seem to be giving way. Mountain chains are sinking. Inhabited islands disappear with their living freight. The seaports that have become like Sodom for wickedness are swallowed up by the angry waters. Great hailstones, every one "about the weight of a talent" (Rev. 16:21), are doing their work of destruction.

The proudest cities of the earth are laid low. The costly palaces, upon which the world's great men have lavished their wealth in order to glorify themselves, are crumbling to ruin before their eyes. Prison walls are rent asunder, and God's people, who have been held in bondage for their faith, are set free.

Graves are opened, and "many of them that sleep in the dust of the earth . . . awake, some to everlasting life, and some to shame and everlasting contempt" (Dan. 12:2). All who have died in faith under the third angel's message come forth from the tomb glorified, to hear God's covenant of peace with those who have kept His law. "They also which pierced him," those that mocked and derided Christ's dying agonies, and the most violent opposers of His truth and His people, are raised to behold Him in His glory, and to see the honor placed upon the loyal and obedient. . . .

Through a rift in the clouds, there beams a star whose brilliancy is increased fourfold in contrast with the darkness. It speaks hope and joy to the faithful, but severity and wrath to the transgressors of God's law. Those who have sacrificed all for Christ are now secure, hidden as in the secret of the Lord's pavilion. They have been tested, and before the world and the despisers of truth they have evinced their fidelity to Him who died for them.

A marvelous change has come over those who have held fast their integrity in the very face of death. They have been suddenly delivered from the dark and terrible tyranny of men transformed to demons. Their faces, so lately pale, anxious, and haggard, are now aglow with wonder, faith, and love. Their voices rise in triumphant song: "God is our refuge and strength, a very present help in trouble. Therefore will not we fear, though the earth be removed, and though the mountains be carried into the midst of the sea; though the waters thereof roar and be troubled, though the mountains shake with the swelling thereof" (Ps. 46:1-3).

While these words of holy trust ascend to God, the clouds sweep back, and the starry heavens are seen, unspeakably glorious in contrast with the black and angry firmament on either side. The glory of heaven is beaming from the gates ajar. Then there appears against the sky a hand holding two tables of stone folded together. The hand opens the tables, and there are revealed the precepts of the Decalogue, traced as with a pen of fire. The words are so plain that all can read them. Memory is aroused, the darkness of superstition and heresy is swept from every mind, and God's ten words, brief, comprehensive, and authoritative, are presented to the view of all the inhabitants of earth. Wonderful code! wonderful occasion! . . .

The voice of God is heard from heaven declaring the day and hour of Jesus' coming, and delivering the everlasting covenant to His people. Like peals of loudest thunder, His words roll through the earth. The Israel of God stand listening, with their eyes fixed upward. Their countenances are lighted up with His glory, and shine as did the face of Moses when he came down from Sinai. The wicked cannot look upon them. And when the blessing is pronounced on those who have honored God by keeping His Sabbath holy, there is a mighty shout of victory. [1]

Soon our eyes were drawn to the east, for a small black cloud had appeared, about half as large as a man's hand, which we all knew was the sign of the Son of man. We all in solemn silence gazed on the cloud as it drew nearer and became lighter, glorious, and still more glorious, till it was a great white cloud. The bottom appeared like fire; a rainbow was over the cloud, while around it were ten thousand angels, singing a most lovely song; and upon it sat the Son of man. His hair was white and curly and lay on His shoulders; and upon His head were many crowns. His feet had the appearance of fire; in His right hand was a sharp sickle; in His left, a silver trumpet. His eyes were as a flame of fire, which searched His children through and through. Then all faces gathered paleness, and those that God had rejected gathered blackness. Then we all cried out, "Who shall be able to stand? Is my robe spotless?" Then the angels ceased to sing, and there was some time of awful silence, when Jesus spoke: "Those who have clean hands and pure hearts shall be able to stand; My grace is sufficient for you." At this our faces lighted up, and joy filled every heart. And the angels struck a note higher and sang again, while the cloud drew still nearer the earth. Then Jesus' silver trumpet sounded, as He descended on the cloud, wrapped in flames of fire. [2]

The earth trembles before Him, the heavens are rolled together as a scroll, and every mountain and every island is moved out of its place. Says the psalmist: "Our God shall come, and shall not keep silence: a fire shall devour before him, and it shall be very tempestuous round about him. He shall call to the heavens from above, and to the earth, that he may judge his people. Gather my saints together unto me; those that have made a covenant with me by sacrifice. And the heavens shall declare his righteousness: for God is judge himself" (Ps. 50:3-6). [3]

Amid the reeling of the earth, the flashing of lightning, and the roaring of thunder, the voice of the Son of God calls forth the sleeping saints. He looks upon the graves of the righteous, then raising His hands to heaven He cries, "Awake, awake, awake, ye that sleep in the dust, and arise!" Throughout the length and breadth of the earth, the dead shall hear that voice, and they that hear shall live. And the whole earth shall ring with the tread of the exceeding great army of every nation, kindred, tongue, and people. From the prison-house of death they come, clothed with immortal glory, crying, "O death, where is thy sting? O grave, where is thy victory?" (1 Cor. 15:55). And the living righteous and the risen saints unite their voices in a long, glad shout of victory.

All come forth from their graves the same in stature as when they entered the tomb. Adam, who stands among the risen throng, is of lofty height and majestic form, in stature but little below the Son of God. He presents a marked contrast to the people of later generations; in this one respect is shown the great degeneracy of the race. But all arise from their last deep slumber with the freshness and vigor of eternal youth.

In the beginning, man was created in the likeness of God, not only in character, but in form and feature. Sin defaced and almost obliterated the divine image; but Christ came to restore that which had been lost. He will change our vile bodies, and fashion them like unto His glorious body. The mortal, corruptible form, devoid of comeliness, once polluted with sin, becomes perfect, beautiful, and immortal. All blemishes and deformities are left in the grave. The redeemed bear the image of their Lord. Oh, wonderful redemption! long talked of, long hoped for, contemplated with eager anticipation, but never fully understood.

The living righteous are changed in a moment, in the twinkling of an eye. At the voice of God they were glorified; now they are made immortal, and with the risen saints are caught up to meet their Lord in the air. Friends long separated by death are united, never more to part. Little children are borne by holy angels to their mothers' arms, and together, with songs of gladness, they ascend to the City of God.

On each side of the cloudy chariot are wings, and beneath it are living wheels; and as the chariot rolls upward, the wheels cry, "Holy," and the wings, as they move, cry,

"Holy," and the retinue of angels cry, "Holy, holy, holy, Lord God Almighty." And the people of God shout "Alleluia!" as the chariot moves onward toward the New Jerusalem. [4]

---

[1] *The Spirit of Prophecy,* vol. 4, pp. 453-458.
[2] *Early Writings,* pp. 15, 16.
[3] *The Spirit of Prophecy,* vol. 4, pp. 459, 460.
[4] *Ibid.,* pp. 463, 464.

CHAPTER NINETEEN

Home at Last!

We all entered the cloud together, and were seven days ascending to the sea of glass. [1]

Before entering the city, the saints are arranged in a hollow square, with Jesus in the midst. In height He surpasses both the saints and the angels. His majestic form and lovely countenance can be seen by all in the square. Upon the heads of the overcomers the Saviour, with His own right hand, places the crowns of glory. For every saint there is a crown, bearing his new name, and the inscription "Holiness to the Lord." In every hand is placed the victor's palm and the shining harp. [2]

Some . . . had very bright crowns, others not so bright. Some crowns appeared heavy with stars, while others had but few. All were perfectly satisfied with their crowns. And they were all clothed with a glorious white mantle from their shoulders to their feet. Angels were all about us as we marched over the sea of glass to the gate of the city. [3]

The commanding angels strike the note, and every voice is raised in grateful praise, every hand sweeps the harp-strings with skillful touch, awaking sweet music in rich, melodious strains. [4]

[Then] Jesus raised His mighty, glorious arm, laid hold of the pearly gate, swung it back on its glittering hinges, and said to us, "You have washed your robes in My blood, stood stiffly for My truth, enter in." We all marched in and felt that we had a perfect right in the city. [5]

Before the ransomed throng is the Holy City. Jesus opens wide the pearly gates, and the nations that have kept the truth enter in. There they behold the Paradise of God, the home of

Adam in his innocency. Then that voice, richer than any music that ever fell on mortal ear, is heard, saying, "Your conflict is ended." The Saviour's countenance beams with unutterable love as He welcomes the redeemed to the joy of their Lord.

Suddenly there rings out upon the air an exultant cry of adoration. The two Adams are about to meet. The Son of God is standing with outstretched arms to receive the father of the race—the being whom He created, who sinned against his Maker, and for whose sin the marks of the crucifixion are borne upon the Saviour's form. As Adam discerns the prints of the cruel nails, he does not fall upon the bosom of his Lord, but in humiliation casts himself at His feet, crying, "Worthy, worthy is the Lamb that was slain!" Tenderly the Saviour lifts him up, and directs his attention to the Eden home from which he has so long been exiled. . . .

Transported with joy, he beholds the trees that were once his delight—the very trees from which he plucked fruit when he rejoiced in the perfection of innocence and holiness. He sees the vines that his own hands have trained, the very flowers that he once loved to care for. His mind grasps the reality of the scene; he comprehends that this is indeed Eden restored, far more beautiful now than when he was banished from it. The Saviour leads him to the tree of life, and plucks the glorious fruit, and bids him eat. He looks about him, and beholds a multitude of his family redeemed, standing in the Paradise of God. Then he casts his glittering crown at the feet of Jesus, and, falling upon His breast, embraces the Redeemer. He touches the golden harp, and the vaults of heaven echo the triumphant song, "Worthy, worthy, worthy is the Lamb that was slain, and lives again!" The family of Adam take up the strain, and cast their crowns at the Saviour's feet as they bow before Him in adoration. [6]

Here we saw the tree of life and the throne of God. Out

of the throne came a pure river of water, and on either side of the river was the tree of life. On one side of the river was a trunk of a tree, and a trunk on the other side of the river, both of pure, transparent gold. At first I thought I saw two trees. I looked again, and saw that they were united at the top in one tree. So it was the tree of life on either side of the river of life. Its branches bowed to the place where we stood, and the fruit was glorious; it looked like gold mixed with silver.

We all went under the tree and sat down to look at the glory of the place. . . . We tried to call up our greatest trials [that we had passed through], but they looked so small compared with the far more exceeding and eternal weight of glory that surrounded us that we could not speak them out, and we all cried out, "Alleluia, heaven is cheap enough!" and we touched our glorious harps and made heaven's arches ring. [7]

The heirs of God have come from garrets, from hovels, from dungeons, from scaffolds, from mountains, from deserts, from the caves of the earth, from the caverns of the sea. But they are no longer feeble, afflicted, scattered, and oppressed. Henceforth they are to be ever with the Lord. They stand before the throne clad in richer robes than the most honored of the earth have ever worn. They are crowned with diadems more glorious than were ever placed upon the brow of earthly monarchs. The days of pain and weeping are forever ended. The King of glory has wiped the tears from all faces; every cause of grief has been removed.

Amid the waving of palm-branches they pour forth a song of praise, clear, sweet, and harmonious; every voice takes up the strain, until the anthem swells through the vaults of heaven, "Salvation to our God which sitteth upon the throne, and unto the Lamb." And all the inhabitants of heaven respond in the ascription "Amen: Blessing, and glory, and

wisdom, and thanksgiving, and honour, and power, and
might, be unto our God for ever and ever" (Rev. 7:10, 12). [8]

---

[1] *Early Writings*, p. 16.
[2] *The Spirit of Prophecy*, vol. 4, p. 464.
[3] *Early Writings*, pp. 16, 17.
[4] *The Spirit of Prophecy*, vol. 4, pp. 464, 465.
[5] *Early Writings*, p. 17.
[6] *The Spirit of Prophecy*, vol. 4, pp. 465, 466.
[7] *Early Writings*, p. 17.
[8] *The Spirit of Prophecy*, vol. 4, pp. 467, 468.